I0752575

AVA'S MAGIC WORD

Sheila Eleven

Published by Shelia Eleven

Stockbridge, GA

ISBN:

Paperback: 979-8-9939053-0-3
Hardcover: 979-8-9939053-1-0
Ebook:979-8-9939053-2-7

First Edition

Printed in United States

Illustrations by: Shalethia Jones (Storyboard Artist) and Mar Fandos (Illustrator)

For more information, visit www.avasmagicworld.com

I dedicate this book to my grandchildren my dearest loves; Michael, Makiyah, Brooklyn, Nico, Drake, Bronx, Ava and Avion. May safety always surround you, in childhood and far beyond.

I enjoy meditation
I love roller blading
I'm a gymnast

I love reading
I love taking pictures
I love science

"Hi! I'm Ava. My friends and I are here to help YOU learn something super important: how to stay safe and protect your body.
"Hello! I'm Levi!"
"I'm Zaina!"
"I am Beiye!"
"Hi! I am Karthik!"
"I am, Bronx! Ava's Brother!"
AVMW
AVMW

Time to go, you guys!

"Today, we're not talking about arms or legs. Not even elbows or ears. We're talking about something extra important—our private parts."

Are you guys ready for some sleepover fun?
Yes!
I am excited!

What are private parts? Special area's on our bodies that no one should touch without permission.
Hurry, girls! Don't forget to head upstairs to put your stuff away and wash up.
AVMW
AVMW

Hey, Dad, we are here!
Hey, I am in the Kitchen. Head upstairs with your stuff!

Girls like me have a vagina. Boys like my brother, Bronx, have a penis. These parts are private. That means they belong only to **YOU**. No one should ever touch your private parts. Not anyone. Not ever. If someone tries, you have the right to say a big, strong **NO!** And then, tell a trusted adult right away.

Snacks are ready downstairs!

You deserve to feel safe everywhere—at Grandma's house, school, church, or even when you're at a friend's sleepover. Feeling safe is your superpower."

Once you roll the dice, just move that many spaces."

That's why my parents and I made a secret magic word. If I ever say it, they know something's wrong, and I need help right away.

My magic word is... Vae Vae.

VAE VAE
VAE
Time for bed.

Do YOU have a magic word with your family? If not, talk with your parent or guardian and make one together! It's like having a superhero signal—just for your safety. We may be kids, but our voices are strong. We are brave. We are the future.

Pearl
ORO
DOUX

"Hey! I'm Bronx. My magic word is Halo. My dad always tells me, "Boys need to protect their private parts, too. I want all the boys out there to be safe, grow strong, and feel proud of who they are."

Goodnight, girls.
Goodnight!
Goodnight!
Goodnight!
AVA

"When we learn how to protect our bodies, we're learning how to be healthy and happy for life! Just like Ava said—create your own magic word with your family. Use it if someone ever makes you feel uncomfortable. And remember: **NO** means **NO**. Always."

NO!
NO!
NO!
NO!
NO!
NO!

Now It's Your Turn! Can YOU think of a magic word with your family? Make it special. Make it a secret. Make it safe. Say it with us, loud and proud:
TOGETHER, WE ARE SAFE!